THE NATIONAL POETRY SERIES

The National Poetry Series was established in 1978 to ensure the publication of five poetry books annually through five participating publishers. Publication is funded by the Lannan Foundation; Stephen Graham; the Joyce & Seward Johnson Foundation; Juliet Lea Hillman Simonds; the Poetry Foundation; Olafur Olafsson; Mr. & Mrs. Michael Newhouse; Jennifer Rubell; the New York Community Trust; Elizabeth Christopherson; and Aristedes Georgantas.

2011 COMPETITION WINNERS

Julianne Buchsbaum, *The Apothecary's Heir*
Chosen by Lucie Brock-Broido

Hannah Gamble, *Your Invitation to a Modest Breakfast*
Chosen by Bernadette Mayer

Juliana Leslie, *Green Is for World*
Chosen by Ange Mlinko

Idra Novey, *Exit, Civilian*
Chosen by Patricia Smith

Marcus Wicker, *Maybe the Saddest Thing*
Chosen by D. A. Powell

D1466617

Exit, Civilian

Exit, Civilian

POEMS BY IDRA NOVEY

THE UNIVERSITY OF GEORGIA PRESS
Athens & London

Published by The University of Georgia Press
Athens, Georgia 30602
www.ugapress.org
Designed by Walton Harris
Set in 10/14 Electra LT Std
Printed and bound by Thomson-Shore
The paper in this book meets the guidelines for
permanence and durability of the Committee on
Production Guidelines for Book Longevity of the
Council on Library Resources.

Printed in the United States of America

16   15   14   13   12   P   5   4   3   2   1

Library of Congress Cataloging-in-Publication Data

Novey, Idra.
Exit, civilian : poems / by Idra Novey.
    p.   cm. — (The National Poetry Series)
Includes bibliographical references.
ISBN-13: 978-0-8203-4348-8 (pbk. : alk. paper)
ISBN-10: 0-8203-4348-X (pbk. : alk. paper)
I. Title.
PS3614.O928E95 2012
811'.6—dc23   2011049717

British Library Cataloging-in-Publication Data available

For the students
in the Bard Prison Initiative,

and for Sara Novey Brozgal,
in whose name I write.

CONTENTS

my heart went white as hair whitens

Then, before understanding, my heart went

ACKNOWLEDGMENTS

Thanks to the editors of the publications and websites where the following poems first appeared, some in slightly different versions.

Academy of American Poets Poem-a-Day: "Parole Hearing"

AGNI: "If Vallejo Hadn't Died in Paris"

American Poetry Review: "The Little Prison"

BOMBLog: "The Little Prison, I"

Catch Up: "Grand Jury, the Sound of Leaves"

Cura: A Literary Magazine of Art and Action: "House Arrest"

Dossier: "On Bafflement," originally published as "Bewilderment"

The New Orleans Review: "The Lava Game" and "The Etymological Beginning," originally published as "Essay"

Loaded Bicycle: "A Maça no Oscuro," originally published as "The Apple in the Dark"

Poets.org: "Parole Hearing"

A Public Space: "The Ex-Cárcel of Valparaíso"

Subtropics: "Meanwhile the Watermelon Seed"

Tongue: A Journal of Writing and Art: "Recent Findings"

Virginia Quarterly Review: "Memorias do Cárcere" and "As Charged"

Women's Studies Quarterly: "Riding By on a Sunday"

Zoland Poetry Annual: "The Little Prison Responds," originally published as "Conditions of Visitation," and "O Caldeirão do Diabo"

The section titles are from a sentence in my forthcoming retranslation of Clarice Lispector's novel *The Passion According to G.H.* (New Directions, 2012).

Great bottomless wells of thanks to the many friends who read this manuscript many times and to my family, near and far. More great bottomless wells of thanks to Patricia Smith for selecting this manuscript for the National Poetry Series, and to Regan Huff and everyone at the University of Georgia Press. *Y gracias a la vida que me ha dado L y B.*

Exit, Civilian

The Little Prison

Enter the little prison a comma
And you come out a question mark

Enter a scallop
And you come out the shell

Enter in English
And you come out murmuring
What your great-grandmother murmured
To other shells
On another shore

Enter an apple
And come out the teeth marks
In its yellowed core

II

The little prison
Has no interest in silence

If you crack a door
It beeps back at you

If you try to read
The Speaker will tell you

Who's collecting garbage
And who's expected on the second floor

And then seven names repeat
For reasons you can't decipher

Until the series of names
Takes on the cadence

And silver radiance
Of prayer

The wet breath
Of its red bricks

Is all the world hears
From the outside

III

There are no hardcover books
For inhabitants of the little prison

They might open them
They might find the lingams of Sai Baba
Or a glimmering orange moon
Which may eclipse and no one
Will alert the little prison

And this is its secret

The little prison was once a field
Herds of deer moved across
And flocks of herons
Their calls rose and echoed

In the spring
If pressed
The little prison that was once a field
Will admit it once likened itself
To the great amphitheater at Delphi

IV

Whisper at the door
Of the little prison
And your voice will become a coin
It will clang and whirl
As if it were in a vacant staircase

Sing at the door
Of the little prison
And your father will tell you
You have stained your shirt

Stand mute
At the door
And your tongue will harden
Like the hoof of a boar

Why come to the door
Of the little prison
When the world is full
Of revolving doors

Do you want to hear more
About the little prison
Have you noticed
It is everywhere

V

Wind a ribbon around the little prison
And pretend you made a gift

Give it to your neighbors
Or your cousins
Clasp your hands
With excitement

Tell them you've been waiting
All week to give them the little prison

At this point you may want
To become an elephant
Or a local expert on weapons

Or simply exit the room

VI

If you have a message for the little prison
The man with the mustache
At the first door before the first hall
Before the first lobby
Will gladly press a button for you
And accept it

And if you have a message
For the man with the mustache
You can give it to his father
Who lives up the river
In the little prison there
Where another man
With another mustache
Sleeps behind another metal desk

You may need
To resend the message

VII

The little prison says it's getting tired
So many inhabitants it says
So many hidden buttons and beeping doors

The little prison says tuck me in
But even the wind is too busy
Papers slip from the giant desk
The little prison closes its eyes

It leans and dreams
Of its little prison hands
Covering its little prison ears
If it could find them

Then, before understanding, my heart went

Civilian Exiting the Facilities

Each week my body is fist-stamped and triple-scanned before it lands again in the electoral world. My mind takes longer to leave, stays in the elevator considering the kind of crime it might be capable of. Would I have to be hungry. Could it happen over nothing. Could it happen nightly. In the shine of a car outside the prison my reflection gets wider until it splits. In one likeness the face I recognize. In the other my face.

Riding By on a Sunday

Nothing shatters.

The day around the prison gleams like the clean face of a spoon.

To the man on the bike beside me, I say, see how it blends in, the same brick and height, disappears after a mile like any other high-rise?

Only A still sits inside, denied parole again for an assault twenty-three years ago.

And Officer M sits in the Annex until ten, stacking the women's ID's according to his ideas of beauty.

The faster we go along the river, the more the city tips into background.

The blocks become ellipses, each building possibly a prison, possibly a warehouse full of pinwheels.

I want to stop longer.

But keep pedaling.

I tell myself prisons are inevitable and inevitably awful.

Tell myself this thought is just another way of looking away.

All day the river beside us streams the silver of dream hair.

Aspect

For the aunt who only ate sugar packets from Applebee's,
we say poor Fay,
who didn't age well.

For the uncle who overdosed on stolen pills, we talk
of good Jerome,
who had too much sorrow.

Of the speeding tickets my father doesn't pay, he says honey,
out of state
may as well be fable.

About the night my mother spent in jail, we say nothing; once
my grandmother said imagine,
your pantyhose stripped in a hallway.

Of the fumbling years, all the waiting for her to look up again,
I say the rub
of my childhood, the thistle.

Overhead

Our flying lessons went over the hour every time. With just a single set of zip-on wings it was a lesson on betting and waiting as much as flight, for surely one of us would understand from the vantage of the sky: how had our local prison expanded more grandly than our fair city, and why? Depending on my stamina I could stay in the air for twenty seconds or

a   full   blue   minute

before I had to do it: flap back to the hilltop or die. Each time I landed I felt clammy and dizzy, having seen little beyond the inside of the zip-on wings we all had to squeeze into and whose synthetic plumage made me sweat profusely.

Parole

I'm going straight to a graveyard, Lena said and Janet said me too, all that grass and no one, a stone bench and some wind—no one belting breakup songs on the radio, no ricochet of shouts just for the sake of it.

In a photo of bones what you notice are the bones: the only things left after the gristle's gone and a voice. To be quiet in a prison, Janet said, is to admit that you're there.

The Little Prison Responds

To witness my insides
Is not so hard

You can come as a prelate of visitations
Or a delegate of the Apostolic See

Come as a wall
A knob
A shatterproof window

Come as a year gone
From every century

As a lamppost snapped
At midnight on the turnpike

Light light light
And then my absence

All Ceremonies Start with Inspection

A dress pressed into a dented metal box. Bodice and satin balled for passage then a passing of body into dress and vestibule and then the picture. After the vows, it all happens again.

Backward—out of the vestibule, out of the dress, a reballing of bodice and back to the far island where the only bread is a photograph, the hands touching in it, wedding band stuck at the knuckle, to stare at that finger as if your eye were a mouth and could eat it.

Meanwhile the Watermelon Seed

On Tuesday, new prisoners arrive.

In late fall, when leaves clog the gutters and their last colors go out like stars, new prisoners arrive.

As another plane pitches upward and a red finch drops for landing.

As fleets of schoolchildren go forth in pursuit of green candy.

At three a.m., when dogs shift position on the bed and stir their owners, who look out and find it's snowing.

In the hour when I call my sister and she empties the dishwasher, new prisoners arrive.

In the hour when drivers click on their headlights and flowers close and fireflies get trapped in jars.

On the evening when I see no one, read nothing, and somehow the hours are gone.

In the sweltering city, where a friend brings a watermelon and we spit its seeds onto the roof of the museum next door and the world seems repairable and temporarily right, new prisoners line up outside a pair of doors, enter one at a time.

Titles in the City Library

Searched for: prisons, U.S.

End of education in: 2
Famous escapes from: 109

Gangrene in: 1
Gangs in, feature films on: 63

Hospitals in: 2
Hulks in, feature films on: 13

Overcrowding in: 1
Ozzy Osbourne in: 7

Stones and: 1
Stonewalling and, see also
Henry Kissinger: 4

white as hair whitens. Then, before understanding

Eighteen Hours of Daylight

A woman offers me a pamphlet called *The Miraculous and You*. We're in a city famous for its glaciers and I say no thank you. A chunk of ice calves into the water and the sound is like a bullet. Later, the same woman is in our restaurant. She offers me the same pamphlet, and I wonder if this will keep happening. My mission is to convert the imprisoned, she says, you wouldn't believe how many are awaiting the Miraculous. Around us, the sound of bullets is still the sound of bullets but also the sound of where we are—ice crashing with a smack into the sea, the melt of eleven thousand years unsettling the water to a startling lazuli blue.

As Charged

At the trial, they said I was guilty of M.

I am.

The M was called a B for lack of A and a recent aversion to Cs.

The judge had silver filigree earrings.

The court reporter was so thin she folded shut like a curtain when she swiveled in her seat.

As for Y, time can split anything into more segments, is the orange of infinite portions.

And the M, I confess, gave me a joy so oily and unlike me I might try it again and again.

House Arrest

When punishment became a picture frame, the state gave our mother a glittering one and some picture wire so she could hover properly on the wall. Neighbors asked if this stillness had been in her before, if we poured our milk differently over our cereal with our mother always fixed there and listening.

After weeks of such inquiries, we said enough and climbed in with her—why not be miserable together? For fun, we picked the glitter off her picture frame. Sometimes we ate it for dinner.

The County Courthouse in the Winter

You can hear it listening the way angels do when we make them open-legged in the snow. If you're held in the county jail in July, you're left to slump there for days, melt like a snowman ogling the ladies from heaven in the yard. To hear the courthouse listening in the winter, you have to go outside, put your body where the snow angel lies. Feel her legs
        widen under
         your warm open legs.
         Feel her cold blank face
      fill your mouth.

The Itinerant

At birth, Verdict's cries pricked the quiet the way stars break the dark. To make him stop, his mother Trial strung him out the window with their underclothes. With time, Verdict learned to cry less often and Trial loved him more. They were homebodies for the most part. Questions left them flummoxed as monkeys without thumbs. For fun, they slammed each other in the manner of hammers against wood.

After a while, Trial started to feel old and told her son to hit the road. He called from everywhere but got no answer. He wrote her letters and dropped them in wells. Once in a while one of them would shine up at him like tinfoil or an eye.

Grand Jury, the Sound of Leaves

A woman kept clicking her pen and saying she was going to kill someone. What she really meant was she wanted a cigarette, the way I said I'm dying of hunger. All morning, we said yes, indict everyone. Others who were not us would deal with the jumbled twine of intent. Outside, the blossoms were popping pinkly in the trees and you could tell the sky must be fair the way we wanted our country. It was a little like hunting to sit this long and listen for something we wouldn't do. The footsteps in a dark scene are not unlike the sound of leaves.

Slide Show

A prison made entirely of glass. And that prison inside a glass building full of glass bison grazing on tiny glass splinters made in a prison upstate with so few windows that the bison decorating this promising new facility refuse to bite down on their tiny abundance of splinters

until no one is looking.

Table for Six

In two chairs sit the victims. In another sits the person who did the worst a person can do to another. The other three chairs contain their mothers. The pages in their menus keep sticking together and smell of bureaus. At last, someone addresses the napkins, which are burning. And the napkins answer: this may be the only table you'll ever know.

Parole Hearing

After Mahmoud Darwish

And they searched her voice, heard the lurch of a bus into the
deep muck of a field.

And they searched the bus, saw the guts of its vinyl seats.

And they searched the guts, smelled the steel springs rusting.

And they searched the rust, tasted nothing but the tips of their
thumbs.

And touching their thumbs to their lips they said well in another
three years.

Before They Came for Us

They met in the woods below our homes, brought their sawed-off shotguns and rusted knives, chucked their crushed Budweisers against the trees and greased their beards. Even their laughter was bad. Even their thick feet filthy in their boots. Did they know about the busted window above our bunk beds, that we'd forgotten to close the garage after we put our bikes away? That time by the creek, did we just pretend to drink the dregs from their cans, or did we sip from them? Did we swallow? Were all of them empty? Was that innocence or the end of it? Was it then we began to sneak into our mother's bed, that we began to watch her sleep?

Hearsay

On the radio I hear something about *the wrongly imprisoned* and unplug the vacuum. But it's just two men discussing *vodka and cinnamon* and I'm in one of those rubbed-out, figurative hours when it's best to exit the house without my glasses to see the street I think I know nearly. Only more clearly now, blurred.

The Little Prison Responds to the City

Your gulls won't come closer here
They cluster on the piers
Their wings neat and folded in
Ready to flap into action
The way napkins do

There is nothing of me
I can unfold that crisply
I'm at odds with everything
The tucked wings of gulls
The lulls in traffic and the cars

My name no larger
Than the head of a dog

Titles in the City Library

Searched for: women's prisons, U.S.

Handcuffed during labor in: 2
Whores in, feature films on: 45

Mental illness in: 3
Witches and spells in: 26

Religious education in: 58
Elimination of college education in,
see also William J. Clinton: 2

Ukeleles in, see also *They Always
Call Us Ladies*: 4

my heart went white as hair whitens

On Bafflement

We drew a prison in the sand and it wouldn't go away.

Not even beneath the foam of the biggest waves.

The torn leg of a starfish clung to the door.

A piece of seaweed clung to the bars over the windows.

The tide came in higher and we thought, So much for the prison.

Somebody asked why did we draw that thing,

And were we growing old watching it this way.

We felt compelled to make love in the sand a few feet off.

Then we drew another one, just to see if we'd make love again.

The Etymological Beginning

This much we know: *pris* is the root of it
and means taken, by way of *prehensio*, a
"taking" related to the prehensile grasp
of primates.

       From prehensio, we come to the flexed
       palms of *penitence*, reverently leading us
       into the arms of *penitentiaries*.

              From a spiral for river, a squiggle
              for snake, four hundred and fifty
              years later prisoners still in a cave.

Recent Findings

After the cells of Louise Bourgeois

I

Studies show the difference between legs and arms is in what tends to come after them: hands or feet. As the difference between teaching in a prison and the Ivy League is a question of attendance and if you can tell the weather from the wall.

II

This tiny spiral staircase in the corner appears to be moving. Some experts say it is not. They say getting a degree in prison is like this.

III

It's not uncommon, doctors concur, that gnawing on a stone while speaking of clauses to a mother and daughter incarcerated in the same prison may lead to the gnawing of that stone to stone.

IV

Recent polls note a breakdown in language when people say incarceration over generations, a hesitation and.

V

Too many enclosures make people cold, new data shows, and when it's cold it's going to be cold. As for the spider, she's feeling for an open seam between the walls.

The Metaphysics of Furniture

I picture wood for the unfinished look of violence—the narrow and
unforgiving walnut chair nobody remembers buying or hauling inside.
Today one of us collapsed in the narrow walnut chair. Our panic spat-
tered so fast there was no way to trap it. *Go, go,* whispered the little
boy who'd built a tent for us and filled it with buttercups and mittens.

The Lava Game

We invented a volcano so it would chase us and erase the backyard empire we called The Land. As the lava got closer, whoever was emperor had to race around the tomato plants and toss the plastic tiara we called The Crown.

Once The Crown was in the air, the rest of us got to dive for it, claw each other's faces if we had to. That the only crown in The Land got stolen every disaster seemed as natural to us as the scabbing-over of skin.

If you fell in the dandelions, that was Lava Death. You had to lie there and die a robber till the next emperor said c'mon, c'mon, everybody get up.

I cried once from too much dying in the dandelions. Limp on the ground, that stillness was enormous, acorns printing into my arms, the other voices growing distant and it would occur to me, *we are children.*

We all died as robbers sometimes; I don't know why the emperor always lived. Just before the lava spilled, invisible and everywhere, whoever had The Crown got to describe it.

And whoever couldn't describe it, died too.

Instead of

Maybe there's another place for us to leave and call that leaving wisdom, call it saw-it-once, call it in-the-absence-of.

As our planet does, we have to revolve around ourselves first and then a sun.

After a sentence behind bars, the smog outside becomes the fog of Eden.

The forgotten ease of getting lost in Eden.

You can hear it still in the hallways outside a civil courtroom, the pacing of our million nights awake and thinking, trying to recall it, where the Garden might have been.

The Little Prison Responds

An air-shape
Like the building hiss
Around a plane on a runway
A place like me

The wind-thinness
That is leaving

If Vallejo Hadn't Died in Paris

I see him arrested on 212th Street in New York, while a whore with a magnificent face looks away and men, mid-poker hand, say, *Ave Maria, why does somebody always have to lose?* With the others in his holding cell, he wakes bluely to more blueness, to a cellmate playing a tube of toothpaste against the metal bars and rats nosing at soup cans in the alley behind the wall.

A man with the wrong look about him is arrested. His name is César. They call him *indio narigón* and he does not resist. The words remind him of Lima, which he's been missing.

Riot

Call lockdown call the lapdogs call for backup and God. Call broken pipes and flood risk what all the guards predicted. Call it overcrowding or cloudburst the undoing of done time. Call the sound what it is: shouting and alive.

Titles in the City Library

Searched for: the formerly incarcerated

Housing and jobs for: 3
Heinous crimes by, films on: 146

Mental illness among: 2
Milk of magnesia and: 4

Voting rights for: 1
Votive candles and government-
issued ham for: 5

Then, before understanding, my heart went

O Caldeirão do Diabo

Crocodile—or just a long rock, a *could-be*.

I've been told a *jacaré* hunts this spillway and if I keep still I'll spot him eventually.

A hint of scaly back breaks the water there—

and then there—

I begin to glean all the possibilities for jaws, teeth . . .

Somebody says there was a prison here, so hot it was called The Cauldron.

Somebody says why bother with ruins, just watch for crocodile.

Every night, a new rain traces the exposed roots of trees, fills the mouths of shoes I keep forgetting outside the door.

In my wet shoes I ask again about the ruins, when a boat will go.

Not yet, the boatmen say, come by tomorrow—

And so I become known, The Foreigner Who Asks Too Much about The Cauldron.

I find myself apologizing to strangers in the language of their island, repeating as a child repeats.

Asking one way and then another, thinking the words may change the answer.

And then more rain.

And then asking again.

Memorias do Cárcere

I

An island of jackfruits and great gaps in electricity. The flicker of lizards across walls and the demolition of a prison so recent everyone still has a version of how it fell — all the birds that exploded out of the trees.

Dozens and dozens, says a woman over the sizzle of a fish.

Hundreds, says a man with a toothpick hoping to take her home.

Their talk of birds turns to inmates.

All murderers, says the woman.

Not even a third, says the man, they were leftists with bony elbows. It was a prison of the times.

The man and woman fall silent. Tiny white crabs skitter back to their holes in the sand.

At least they could roam the beaches, says the woman.

A bedtime story, says the man.

II

So lush here, Graciliano, this lizard
island where you were imprisoned.
Every night the lightning strikes more
jackfruits out of the trees and the air
sugars with their smell as they shatter
into the jungle, petaling over the cells
you were locked in for novels none of
your prosecutors could name.

As for your inmates, their bones grow
lighter in a lost grave, but anyone can
tell you where the cobras nest, which
trails lead to beaches and to trees
where the spider monkeys sing.

When I go on here about paradise,
I mean no disrespect. I say it for the
flicker of lizards on the windowsill and
the night smell of jackfruit, for this
much wildness just sixty miles from
Rio.

Enough lushness to erase everything
that's not green or dengue fever,
mosquito or sky.

Fist and After, El Cinzano

The blow came from behind, cracked his nose, and various colors thudded in his eye. His hands cupped the blood. We doubled a towel, yelled *herido*. I thought ER and x-ray. But who was it, people said, didn't someone report it? They wanted—and we did—an *Antes* to the story, some verity of beginning to give clarity to *El Fin*.

Dear stranger, dear anger, dear fantasies of justice, please ferry us to the lake where the stories are clear.

A Maça no Oscuro

What goes missing in this story is not a weapon but the crime. A fugitive arrives at a farm in the far Sertão of Brazil. The two lonely sisters who live there and have never left it say yes, sir—some help with our hens and the broken fence there would be fine. A few apples fall. The corn grows taller. The man sweeps out the silo and a brightness seeps into the sisters—their hands assuming new meanings in the simple opening of canisters, their manicured fingers feeling around the sides. When the police arrive with a description, one sister flinches. The other closes her eyes. Only one has to say it: *Deus meu, he's in our barn.*

The Guest

After Camus's "L'hôte"

The desert police ask the teacher for a favor.

He's to deliver a man who committed a murder to the city police, who will hang him.

But this isn't what happens next.

The teacher gestures, tells the man which dunes will deliver him to the city where the other police are waiting.

Then the teacher gestures toward the south, where the man could also go, and where nomads hold trials of their own.

But I'm telling this story poorly.

First come the regions of France on the teacher's blackboard, none with a desert like this one.

And what follows in the house, the nothing-hours that so often are everything.

The man and the teacher growing larger in the caught breath of a small kitchen.

The yellow smell of eggs turning into a warm cake on the sill.

In the morning, a new muted line tells the desert to the dunes.

A plume of light grows old over the plateau.

Here is where the teacher gestures into the desert.

Here is where the man hesitates, and it's like having his hand in your own.

Then the man chooses the city, the police who await him.

The teacher his school.

On the board between the chalk rivers of France, someone has left him a message: *you will pay for this.*

But it's a chalkboard.

All it takes to start again is water.

A sponge.

The Ex-Cárcel of Valparaíso

And so it was agreed the empty prison would be reopened for festivals, that a pony would be tethered to a table and children would pay for rides along the walls.

The same hour, off in the pampas, a llama was found trotting among the horses and an astrologer in Santiago saw the cosmic future in the crushed bristles of a toothbrush.

At the very same minute at the prison a man began to tune his cello in one of the emptied cells and someone else limped past with timpani drums and children started to follow, children, somebody said, who would in time build a prison of their own, and maybe empty it, maybe fill it again—

The Last Beep and Door

I hold my breath, step into the wet mouth of November wind, arrive at the river moving up and down in its rocky bed, the new art museum that blinks its watery eye. I line up with the others waiting for the M23 bus, which stops for us and we enter it, have the pleasure of choosing whether to sit or stand, which tan and blue-rimmed seat, which window and moving view.

And the ride begins, gradual as a carousel. And all of us inside take on that carousel stillness, as if forty invisible horses were beneath us, and lifting.

NOTES

"The Little Prison" is a response to Vasko Popa's series "The Little Box" as translated by Charles Simic in *Homage to the Lame Wolf*, Oberlin College Press, 1987.

"*Memorias do Cárcere*" is the title of Brazilian novelist Graciliano Ramos's three-volume prison memoir about his time in Cândido Mendes prison after his arrest in 1936 for Communist activities.

"*O Caldeirão do Diabo*," the Devil's Cauldron, is the name inmates and their visitors used for the Cândido Mendes prison on Ilha Grande. The prison was demolished in 1994 and turned into a marine-biology center for students from Rio de Janeiro.

"*A Maça no Oscuro*" is after Brazilian writer Clarice Lispector's novel available in English as *The Apple in the Dark*, translated by Gregory Rabassa.